Make Money Using the Internet to Build a Second Income and Create your Own Business

27 Ways to Earn Extra Money and Sell Merchandise and Services on the Web

Richard G Lowe, Jr

Make Money Using the Internet to Build a Second Income and Create your Own Business

27 Ways to Earn Extra Money and Sell Merchandise and Services on the Web

Earn Money from Your Home Series #3

Published by The Writing King
www.thewritingking.com

Make Money Using the Internet to Build a Second Income and Create your Own Business

Copyright © 2016 by Richard G Lowe, Jr.

Cover Artist: theamateurzone

Library of Congress Control Number: 2016919793

ASIN: B01M1AKGPM
ISBN: 978-1-943517-67-1 (Hardcover)
ISBN: 978-1-943517-66-4 (Paperback)
ISBN: 978-1-943517-38-1 (eBook)

Table of Contents

Table of Contents

Introduction

Everyone needs a little extra money sometimes – that is unless they happen to be multimillionaires or win the lottery or something. But if you're anything like me, earning a few extra dollars from home is a great way to get a little ahead on the bills, save up for a vacation, or just have a buffer and perhaps a bit in savings.

These days, even in homes that have two wage earners, it can be very difficult to get ahead on income that comes from salaries. After taxes, rent or mortgage, utilities, the kids, and all the other things that pile up from day-to-day, there often doesn't seem to be much left to spend on anything else.

The Internet can be a great place to help with the problem of getting ahead financially. There are literally millions of ways to make money, far more than was ever imaginable just a decade or two ago.

On the other hand, scams are everywhere, and there are people who want to convince you they have the answer for your moneymaking dreams. All you have to do is give them $9.95, $197, $10,000 or some other amount, and they will spill their guts and tell you the secrets to earning extra cash by the bucket load with little to no effort.

It can be difficult to discern what is real from what is a scam or a passing fad. Sometimes moneymaking websites and email offerings are very slick and can be extremely convincing. This is especially true when the price is low because it seems that for just a few dollars the risk that it's a

Introduction

scam is worth it. After all, isn't there a chance that spending $9.95 to get ten thousand dollars actually works? Wouldn't you be a fool to pass up on that kind of offer?

I've been making money on the Internet for going on fifteen years now. I haven't made a fortune, but I have eked out a few extra dollars, sometimes a few thousand at a time. I've tried many different things and run into quite a few scams. Unfortunately, I fell for a few of them and wound up losing money here and there. Each time, though, I became a little wiser and bit less gullible.

Over that same span of years, I've been lucky enough to have made far more money than I lost. After a while, the scams become easier to spot, since most of them follow an annoyingly similar pattern.

I found a few things that do work, and that's really the difference between an offer that's a scam and one that's valid. The scam promises you incredible riches for very little work. Programs that are valid don't make that offer; instead, they tell you right up front that their program is going to take effort, time, money, creativity, and elbow grease.

As with most businesses, you have to put in the energy to get back income. If someone offers you a way to make money, especially significant amounts of money, with little to no work, then it's almost certainly a scam of one sort or another.

Sometimes someone will figure out a way to make money then create a product which tells other people, using videos, slideshows, and PDF files, how to re-create their success. The problem with these is usually these individuals were lucky or stumbled onto a fad. These quickly fade away as the public loses interest, and those people who buy into the project later in the game don't tend to make much money (if any at all.)

The difference between doing business on the Internet in the modern world and trying to make a living a decade ago is that the entire planet is literally at your fingertips. This means that you can sell products and services to people in Saudi Arabia, Pakistan, Europe, the United States and anywhere else.

This is especially true for selling services, because with physical products you have to deal with shipping, customs agents and so forth. But for services you can use the Internet in its entirety to deliver value to your customers.

For example, one of my jobs is to write LinkedIn profiles for a company called LinkedIn Makeover, and for this, I have to do two interviews for each person who signs up for the service. The interviews are done using Skype because Skype-to-Skype communications are free of charge. The product, a completed LinkedIn profile, is delivered over the web, which makes it easy and doesn't involve physically crossing borders. Even payment is done using online banking services that take care of exchange rates and other things that would normally be complex for an individual.

Additionally, you can take advantage of online storefronts such as Amazon, EBay, CafePress, and thousands of others to sell products and services without worrying about delivery and payment.

EBay has an option which makes this particularly straightforward. You specify that international sales should

Introduction

ship using their global shipping option, which means that you are responsible only for getting it to an EBay office which then handles all of the customs documents that are required by the destination country. This means that all of the details associated with shipping to a hundred different countries all over the planet are not your concern.

If you have a skill you can easily start a business from home and rather quickly make a living at it. Websites such as Fiverr and Upwork and so on allow you to offer your services to anyone for a fee. The website takes care of payment for you, so all you need to be concerned with is creating and delivering the finished product.

Even your hobbies can be the seed for small Internet businesses. Etsy and CafePress are great places for you to create merchandise that you enjoy and can resell them to other people.

Even if all you have to offer is your time, you can find ways to make money doing things for other people. By setting yourself up as a virtual assistant, you can charge $10, $15, or even $20 per hour or more to help people with their needs. I use virtual assistants occasionally to do research, fill in forms, compile lists, and perform other mundane tasks so that I can focus on activities that create income.

One of the big advantages to using an established website such as EBay, Amazon, CafePress, and so on is they will pay directly into your checking account or use a service such as PayPal. They even send you the tax documents that you need each year in order to give the government its share of your money.

If you have a different frame of mind, you can create a blog and use it to generate income. You can make money off of a blog by listing banner ads and other forms of advertising. Your blog can also generate income by promoting products, giving you a percentage of each sale. Alternately, you can advertise your own products and services.

Each of the options available to create income on the web comes with a series of trade-offs. Established websites with very large audiences such as Amazon and EBay demand relatively high fees yet provide services to make sales trivial. One of the big advantages to these sites is they perform much of the marketing for you. In other words, they already have an established customer base and your task is to list your products in such a way that others are attracted to them.

Most other moneymaking opportunities require that you gain a certain amount of skill at marketing. You have to use various methods to get people to your blog or your products on Etsy or CafePress.

Marketing your product or service is often the stumbling block for many entrepreneurs on the web. For example, there are products available which will teach you how to "write a book in three hours," "create a new and exciting product in less than a day," and so on. All of these tend to fail on one point — getting people to purchase, or even to see that product or service that you worked so hard on.

Introduction

As an example, I purchased a product for around ten bucks which detailed how to create a Sudoku puzzle book in just a few hours. It's a fantastic idea but the problem is that a thousand other people bought the product and created their own Sudoku puzzle books for sale on Amazon. How do you make your Sudoku book stand out from the crowd? How do you get people to see your page among the ten or twenty thousand other pages promoting what is essentially the same product?

Thus, when evaluating whether to spend the money on a new venture or moneymaking scheme always ask yourself the question "how am I going to market this?" For the Sudoku books, a quick search on Amazon uncovered that there are literally thousands of these, most of them essentially the same. To make matters worse they all get very few sales.

Even on those websites, such as Amazon and EBay, which do much of the marketing for you, you have to spend the time to create good product description pages. These include photos, an enticing description of the product, a headline, and information to make it easy for customers to find your items or services. The quality of a photo can mean the difference between selling your item quickly or having it sit there for six months.

In this book, I've chosen 27 different ways to make money on the Internet. This is by no means all of the methods available — there are literally millions of different options and websites that you can explore.

I've actually made money, or personally know people who have created an income, from each of these different services.

I'm one of those lucky people who works from home and makes a pretty good living at it. I am my own boss, and at the end of the day, the person who is responsible for whether or not I make it as an entrepreneur is myself.

My success is dependent on the quality of the products and services that I offer combined with how well I market those so that other people can find them and make a decision as to whether or not to purchase.

It's actually a very good life. It's quite common for me to spend half the day in my pajamas since the first thing I do when I get up is to start writing or working on a product.

For thirty-three years I worked in corporate America, spending twenty of those at Trader Joe's. I left that world because I wanted to work for myself and reap the benefits of my skills, intelligence, and creativity.

I found when you work for someone else you get a paycheck, some benefits, and the comfort of being part of an organization. It seems that most people like this kind of structure and the illusion of safety.

No matter how safe you believe you are in your job, you are at risk from the whims of other people in the organization.

Your boss might be the nicest and most competent person on the planet, and your organization might value your services

Introduction

and your contributions. Even so, all of that can change overnight.

One day everything is rosy, and the next, a new boss may come on board and decide, for no apparent reason, that you need to go. Or the company may change its direction or leadership, and you may be one of the unlucky recipients of a layoff notice via email.

Working for yourself has its own set of difficulties, the most significant of which is it's up to you to find ways to make income and to turn those into actual money producing ventures. Usually, that process is not quick; if you expect to quit your job today and make a living at selling things on EBay tomorrow, that's very unlikely to happen.

You'll need to take the time to build up your business, figure out your niche or passion, and turn it into something that creates a living for you. Be prepared for this to take one, two or more years, and be ready to change direction if needed at any time.

I started my freelance writing career with the idea that I was going to write some books and sell them on Amazon. In order to make a living in the meantime, I offered my services as professional ghostwriter and blogger, which is not something that I would've predicted. To help fill in some of the gaps in income, I began selling things on EBay and Amazon and explored many of the options discussed within this book.

This is a summary of my experiences producing income on the Internet. In each chapter I'm going to describe one method for generating income, explain how it works briefly, and discuss the pros and cons as well as the opportunities.

The idea is to give you an understanding of the immense variety of opportunities that are available to you so that you can choose the ones that make sense for your situation.

I think the most exciting thing about being able to work on the Internet is that it's global and the scope is vast. It's quite possible for you or anyone to be able to produce something you are passionate about, as opposed to just working a 9-to-5 job for the man.

I hope this book gives you some ideas about how you can pursue your passion, earn some extra money to help you with your finances, and perhaps even make you less reliant on a full-time job working for some big corporation.

I hope you enjoy what I've written and find it to be of some value. If you would like to send me a note about this book, feel free to write me at rich@thewritingking.com. If you enjoyed the book, please write a positive review.

A Note about Scams and Frauds

The Internet is a wild place. In some ways, it makes the wild, wild West look tame. If you're not careful, you could find yourself being robbed by a bandit, ambushed by criminals, or lost in the desert.

The slick websites such as Amazon and EBay make it appear that the Internet is completely safe. As long as you stick to those larger, more established sites, you are correct.

But if you're actively searching or poking around, especially if you're looking for ways to make money, you could easily fall victim to malicious individuals, evil corporations, and scams of all sorts.

Before you begin your online search for things that you can do to produce income, make sure that the security on your computer is up to date. You can pick up a copy of my book _Safe Computing is Like Safe Sex_, if you'd like to get details about how to make sure your Windows system is relatively secure.

The Internet is rife with scams, and sometimes they are very difficult to spot. There are thousands of people just looking for suckers, and as the saying goes, "there is a sucker born every minute."

Watch out for pyramid schemes. These are "money making" programs which promise great riches, and all you need to do is sell the program itself to other people. Supposedly, you make income off your sales of the so-called product or

A Note about Scams and Frauds

service, plus any sales made by those further "down" who sell the scheme. The key point to look out for is that there is really no product, although sometimes these schemes camouflage that to make to look like they provide a valuable service. The only people who get rich off of pyramid schemes are those at the top of the pyramid. The further down you get, the less money you make, and the ones near the bottom wind up actually losing money. Stay away from them. Note that pyramid schemes are illegal.

A few months ago, I received an email that advertised a course that cost $7 which claimed that I could make thousands of dollars a month just by following their instructions. The video was very persuasive and explained that it had to do with adding certain kinds of advertisements to YouTube videos.

I was intrigued, so I paid the seven bucks. As is common for moneymaking programs, whether or not they're legitimate, I was immediately offered an upsell, which is an attempt to get a buyer to purchase another product, usually for more money.

I didn't buy the upsell, but once I clicked the button saying no, I was sent to another one, and then another, for a total of twenty-seven of them, which is beyond ridiculous. Once I actually got into the program's website, I discovered that the product was actually the series of upsells that I had just navigated. In other words, I was expected to sell this pyramid scheme to other people who would pay the $7 and probably one or two of the upsells, and I would receive a commission based on that.

A Note about Scams and Frauds

This scam did promote a service, which was some kind of worthless series of videos talking about how to add advertisements to other people's YouTube videos. It was pretty obvious this so-called course was included to obscure the scam.

That's a pretty classic pyramid scheme. Since it had disguised itself is legitimate product up front, I was fooled, but fortunately I only lost $7.00.

Another common occurrence (not always a scam) happens when somebody figures out a way to make money that works for them. They write it up as a product and sell it, usually via several very large email marketing groups.

The way this works is you receive an invitation to a webinar, which is an online course, usually taking about an hour, similar in format to an infomercial. The webinar promises that you will receive some tips, secrets or advice that's of extreme value, and they may even put a dollar amount on that to make it appear even more enticing.

These webinars are often valuable by themselves. They spend forty-five minutes giving useful information related to whatever product or service they are attempting to sell.

Near the end, inevitably, comes the attempt to get you to purchase a product, service or course. After all, the webinar is the hook to get you excited and anxious to buy. Sometimes these products have some value, and perhaps 90% of the time they are worthless or worse.

A Note about Scams and Frauds

I used to attend these regularly, sometimes three or four a week, until I realized that there mostly a waste of time. Oh sure, they do give out a few tips and you sometimes have the opportunity to ask some questions, but once you get beyond the beginner level these webinars have little value. Not only that, the endless stream of emails and the hard-sell that occurs, as a result, can get very tiring and annoying.

If you are going to buy in to purchasing their offer, make sure they clearly state that there is a money back guarantee with no conditions. This should be mentioned by them sometime during the webinar and it should be clearly indicated on the website where they'll send you to purchase the product.

Keep in mind that some of these offerings charge monthly, quarterly or yearly recurring fees, which makes the cost higher than you might think.

Once you've made your purchase, be sure to check it out immediately. Generally, these products are either PDF files with a few videos, or they are online courses with membership websites. As soon as you get the password, download the product or log into the website and take a look around. Review the materials, and if possible, immediately put whatever program they're promoting to work.

If it turns out that the product is garbage or sub-optimal, isn't what you thought it was, or the program doesn't work, then ask for your money back and don't take any excuses. All of the legitimate programs will give your money back right away.

Also, wait to purchase any upsells if at all possible. The problem with upselling is that you really don't know what you're getting.

Here's how it works: you purchase a product for $27, which is a very common price. Immediately after you make your payment, usually via PayPal, you'll be sent to another page that thanks you for ordering and then presents you with lots of details about a more advanced version or a bonus offer or something of that nature. You'll be told that you need to purchase that immediately because this is your only chance or it will be offered to you at a higher price later.

These upsells are frequently costlier than the first product you purchased. If you do decide to buy the upsell, make sure the page clearly indicates that it also has a money back guarantee.

Once you purchase the upsell, you'll frequently be sent to a third page which has yet another upsell for an even more dazzling and wonderful product. It's quite common for both legitimate and scam products and services to follow this exact same pattern.

The idea is since you're caught up in the moment, and you are excited from all of the information presented in the webinar, you're a bit vulnerable and can be pushed into making more purchases. You'd be amazed at the number of people who purchase the upsell – that's often where the authors of these programs make their real money.

That's not to say that these webinars have no value and everything they sell is garbage or scams. They often give a lot

A Note about Scams and Frauds

of useful information by themselves – especially for beginners – and the advertised products may deliver exactly what they promise.

Several of the products and courses advertised in webinars helped me get a start in my writing career. Some of these were very valuable — in fact, two of them form the basis for my success.

As you sit through these webinars or review the marketing information that you received an email, you will have to use your own best judgment.

Does it appear to be too good to be true? Are you being offered to receive riches or large amounts of money for little or no work?

Making money on the Internet virtually always requires that you put in some serious effort and work. If you are being offered a way to make money which requires "only three hours work" or "three days to make $2,000 a month," then you're probably being scammed.

I'll give you some examples of what I found. I'm a writer and I'm always looking for interesting ways to make money by producing books that people want to buy.

One program consisted of a class to create puzzle books which would "just sell themselves" because, according to the author, they were that popular. He claimed the books would take three hours to create, probably another hour to publish, and then you were done and, after that, it was just a matter of sitting back and waiting for the money to roll in.

A Note about Scams and Frauds

I created several of them and actually was able to publish them with less than three hours of effort. The problem was the marketing; which is common among many of these programs. It's very rare that any book "sells itself." You virtually always need to put time and money into marketing. This means you need to create an email list, build a high-traffic website, or purchase paid advertisements. In other words, the product might be simple to create, but the marketing is complex and quite possibly expensive.

In another case, the product gave a method for creating interview books in just a few hours. The author claimed that these books would sell like hot cakes on Amazon.com.

I'm sure you know the story by now. I went ahead and created a few of them, and they do indeed take very little time. However, they don't "just sell themselves." In actuality, they're very difficult to market, and I've sold less than a dozen of the ones that I produced. In other words, it was not a great return on investment. In fact, the money I earned wouldn't even have paid for the course. I asked for and received a refund on the product.

When looking at a product or service that you are considering to purchase, ask yourself these questions:

Does it seem too good to be true?

Is the marketing side of things included?

Does it come with a no questions asked money back guarantee?

A Note about Scams and Frauds

Is everything included or do you need to purchase one or more up sells to make it valuable or complete?

Is the product claiming that you can make large amounts of money with very little effort and time?

Are you really going to take the time to produce and sell as per their instructions, or are you just caught up in "buyers fever?"

Once you have the answers to these questions, make your decision. If the webinar requires that you make a purchase before the end, use caution and ensure you have a money back guarantee. If you can, give yourself an extra day or two to calm down from the excitement of learning new things and being hit with a hard sell before making a decision.

Use your good judgment, and don't purchase based on an emotional reaction. That usually turns out to be a bad idea.

Affiliate Sales

If you want to make money on the Internet, you can do so by becoming an affiliate for products that you resell. What this means is you earn a commission each time you responsible for the sale of a product. Sometimes those commissions are just a few percent, and sometimes you get paid as much as half the total cost or even more.

The way it works is someone creates a product — it could be a corporation or an individual — and then sets up an affiliate program for it. People such as yourself use a special hyperlink - known as an affiliate link - to send traffic to an affiliate website. If a sale results, you get a commission.

In essence, affiliate marketing is a way to gain a motivated sales force. It's a good exchange — they sell their product and make income, and you help them sell it and make a little money for yourself.

Pros

If you've already got marketing channels set up, or you enjoy salesmanship, then affiliate marketing should be relatively simple for you. With a good mailing list or a high-traffic website, you can potentially earn quite a bit of income.

You can be in more than one affiliate program, and advertise many products on your blog or in your email list. Using this method, you can expand your income even further.

Affiliate Sales

Cons

Selling products or services requires marketing expertise. In order to make a significant amount of money, you need a large mailing list or very high traffic blog or website. Without the traffic — by any means — you may make a sale now and then, bringing an extra few dollars, but you won't be able to make a living at it.

Conclusions

There's absolutely no reason why you can't join as many affiliate programs as you want. In fact, whenever you purchase a product that's related to your niche, you should check to see if there is an affiliate program available. If there is, there is no harm in signing up for it. You can then write articles for your blog or email list which promote the product.

It's a good way to make a few extra dollars without a lot of extra work.

Of course, if you do have a large email list or another way to gain a lot of traffic, you could earn some real money.

Amazon

One of the easiest ways to make money on the Internet is to list your products on Amazon.com. You can sell almost anything on Amazon, from traditional books to electronics, toys, games, and movies. Their selling platform is straightforward for the beginner but has options for the power user to make life simpler and selling and shipping more efficient.

To get started selling on Amazon, you need an Amazon account. If you have ever purchased anything from them, you almost certainly have one of these. Create a seller account from within the account management screen of your Amazon account.

Once you have your seller account, you can start entering products. I began by entering books that I wanted to get rid of. Amazon makes this very simple. Enter the title, author, ISBN number or other identifying value to get a list of matching products from Amazon's catalog. Use this to create your listing, set a price, and fill in all the details.

One caveat about shipping — Amazon sets all shipping to $3.99 (with some exceptions), regardless of how much it costs to actually ship the product. This amount is intended to pay for the postage, shipping container, packing materials and everything else needed to get the product to the customer. This is why you'll find products for sale on Amazon for a penny or a dime — the seller is counting on the fact that the shipping charge will give them a small profit.

Amazon

Amazon's basic service assumes that you're going to ship these products yourself, which entails keeping an inventory, boxing up the product, dropping it off the post office, and handling any returns or refunds yourself.

More advanced users can use the FBA service to ship all of their products at once to Amazon, where they are stored in a warehouse. Amazon takes care of shipping these products to the customer automatically without intervention. Of course, a fee is charged for the service.

Pros

Amazon has one of the most complete and straightforward selling platforms available anywhere on the Internet. For items that already exist in Amazon's catalog, selling is extremely convenient and simple. This platform is an excellent way for someone to make extra money selling things that they already own, or by using drop shipping or other methods.

Cons

Amazon's fees are extraordinarily high, especially for the FBA service. You must be very careful to take into account shipping charges and Amazon's charges in order to ensure that you make a profit on your items. On several occasions, I was dismayed to find that I actually took a loss when I sold a product.

To my knowledge, Amazon does not provide phone support. You must ask your questions via their contact form, after navigating a complex set of menus which attempts to give you answers to standard questions. This can make it very frustrating if your problem is not "normal" or if it's urgent.

For many products, such as books, the competition can be very high, making it difficult to get a sale. On numerous occasions, I found dozens of other sellers offering their products for pennies, which made it impossible for me to match and still make a profit. Since buyers often purchase based upon price, this means if your product is not among the lowest, it will sit in the Amazon store for quite a while before someone makes a purchase, if it sells at all.

Conclusions

Selling products such as books, electronics, games and so forth via Amazon is extraordinarily simple. The fees can be high, and you have to be very aware of the shipping costs, but Amazon is an excellent place to gain experience at selling products online, especially if you have items that you already own that you want to sell.

Amazon Associates

A cool way to make money is to set yourself up as an Amazon Associate, which more or less means that you are an affiliate for Amazon. This is very simple: log into your Amazon account and look for the link that says sign up to be an Amazon Associate. Click it, fill in the blanks, and when you're done you're accepted into the program.

You have about three months to make your first sale, and if you don't meet the quota your account will be canceled. This is nothing to worry about, as you can create another one with a different ID easily and try again.

Use your affiliate account whenever you sell Amazon products. For example, if you created a book review site, you could add your Amazon associate ID to the book sales links and each time someone bought a book, you would get a small commission.

It's very simple to add your ID to product links. An example is shown below.

https://www.amazon.com/dp/1537223232/?tag=thewritingkin -20

The part of the link that is the affiliate ID is everything after the ?tag. In this case, my affiliate ID is thewritingkin-20, so I add "?tag=thewritingking-20" to each Amazon link.

The factor that makes this even more powerful is by including your affiliate ID on a link, you get a commission on ALL of the sales made by that buyer during a browsing session. Thus, if someone who clicks on your book link goes to Amazon but decides not to buy the book, then purchases a dozen movies, you get a small commission on that sale of all those movies. It doesn't matter whether or not they purchase the product that you are advertising.

Pros

This is a very easy way to make a few extra dollars, especially if you are selling books or other products of your own through Amazon. You can include your affiliate link and increase your income.

Cons

There is no reason not to do this, as it will add extra money to your income without any downside. Don't expect to make a fortune, but you might get a few extra dollars now and then.

Conclusions

Join the Amazon Associates program and use your associate ID on any link that you make to Amazon, including a link straight to the homepage. It's easy money, especially if you have an existing website, email list or book.

Amazon Mechanical Turk

If you've got some time and you don't mind working on mindless tasks, check out Amazon Mechanical Turk. This website, owned by Amazon, allows individuals to work from home, choose their own working hours, and select tasks that they can complete for a small fee.

The tasks are simple and quick and include such things as selecting the correct spelling for the search term, looking over a website to make sure that it's suitable for a general audience, determining if two products are the same or even translating a paragraph from one language into another.

The idea is that the jobs are supposed to be quick and easy, yet need to be done by a human being. The pay for each task is very low, sometimes a penny, but it's all simple and easy so they can be done quickly.

You're not going to make a lot of money using this system, but as long as you're quick and to the point, you may be able to earn some extra cash which could be very helpful.

Pros

Tasks are simple and quick. Many of them take just a few seconds. A determined person could do several per minute or hundreds per hour. This will not make you a huge amount of money, but it's more productive than watching television or laying on the couch.

Amazon Mechanical Turk

Cons

You won't make a lot of money, and the tasks are boring and mundane.

Conclusions

This is a great opportunity to make a few dollars while you're looking for other things that generate more income. You can keep the screen open and do one of their tasks such as searching online for jobs, watching television, or other boring and mundane tasks.

Banner Ads

In the early days of the Internet, banner ads and other forms of advertising were the rave. The Internet was new and shiny and advertising had not yet been oversaturated; in other words, you could put up a banner, and there was reasonable chance that some people would click on it.

This was because it was new and people were not yet overwhelmed with the noise, and thus hadn't built up a tolerance to viewing ads.

In those days, it wasn't uncommon for there to be one click for every ten or twenty impressions of an advertisement. Today, due to the massive number of ads for everything, the ratio has changed to more like one click in a thousand or even one in ten thousand impressions.

In other words, it takes a lot more eyeballs to generate clicks on advertisements. Not only that, advertisements must be fancier, with expensive graphics, animation, movies, and hundreds of other gimmicks just to get more people to see them, much less click on the box and perhaps make a purchase.

In the early days of the Internet, advertising companies often paid based on the number of impressions, or viewings, of an advertisement. That model no longer works, and you'll have difficulty finding anyone who pays based upon impressions.

Today, most advertising companies pay based upon a number of clicks, which is the number of times that people actually clicked on an advertisement through to an advertising page of some kind.

Additionally, it is often possible to get revenue based on the purchase of products, which is described in the Affiliate Marketing section of this book.

Pros

Implementing banner ads are as simple as signing up for various advertising services, such as CJ.com, and adding those banners to your blog and other places.

Cons

Adding banner ads to a blog is often one of the first moneymaking attempts by a newbie to Internet moneymaking. It seems so easy, and the allure is great. If you can get the traffic, you'll make money.

Conclusions

Making more than a few pennies a month from banner ads is difficult because it requires generating huge amounts of traffic, a large investment in paid advertising or the use of email marketing. Even so, it is worth the time to add a banner ad to your site since, once added, no further effort is needed.

Additionally, many people these days are using ad blockers to remove banner ads entirely, so a large portion of your audience will never even see the fruits of your labor.

Blogging

One way to make money on the Internet is to create a blog. Your blog can generate an income directly, by selling products and posting banner ads, and indirectly by supporting your brand.

I look at my blog as the center of my Internet world. You could call it my home or home base so to speak. This is where I publish my articles, create a page for each of my books, post about the services I offer, and is a place to put my business card and promotional materials.

By doing this, my blog indirectly helps me promote my business and thus reinforces my income-producing abilities.

The art of creating targeted traffic is the ability to attract the attention of influencers who will send visitors your way. If you can find a high-traffic website and pitch a guest blog to them, which they publish, you can potentially receive a large spike of visitors. Keep doing this over and over, and your blog will gain that targeted traffic.

Another method is to use paid advertisements, such as Google AdSense, or to maintain a very active and large email list. Creating effective paid advertisements and building an email list is a huge subject beyond the scope of this book. Suffice to say that in each of these instances, it's best to hire a professional unless you already have experience in the area.

Blogging

Pros

If you do want to create a blog that generates income, you need to become an expert at gaining the attention of influencers, building an email list or using paid advertisements.

You can create an income stream from your blog, but it requires a lot of work and a strong focus on generating traffic. If you treat your blog as a full-time job, get the appropriate training from reliable sources, and remain focused it's possible that you can, after several years, find yourself making a tidy sum of money.

Cons

A blog that is outdated is worse than useless as it can actually discourage people from buying your products or services. Keeping a blog up to date requires diligence and a lot of work.

Blogs work best when they support your brand; it's difficult to make money off advertisements unless you can get large amounts of traffic.

Conclusions

A blog is best when used as a home base for your Internet business. Use it as a place to show off your talents, your services, and your products. Additionally, by printing the address on your business cards and stationery, you provide a place where people can go to find out more about you, your products and your services.

CafePress

If you've got some ideas for creating products such as coffee mugs, T-shirts, calendars and so forth, then CafePress might be your perfect solution.

For example, if you are a photographer or an artist, you can use Café press to create calendars containing your work which you can then sell. CafePress has a long list of different types of merchandise that you can create, including iPhone cases, mugs, posters, stationery and even drinking glasses.

The real beauty of their program is that everything is created on demand, which means that you do not need to pay any money upfront to get your products designed and sold. All you need to do is create an account, then use their tools to create your unique and interesting products.

You'll have to market those products yourself using techniques such as email lists, highly trafficked websites, and paid advertisements. But CafePress makes the creation of your products simple and straightforward.

CafePress also has more advanced options for you to create storefronts and fan based websites. This allows you to build a whole shop full of products that you can sell.

Pros

It's easy to create products using the tools provided online by CafePress. Those products are created on demand so no money is needed upfront. Additionally, the products are high quality and all of the shipping and collection of money is done for you.

Cons

CafePress has a limited number of products that can be created and those products don't have many variations. Additionally, very little marketing is provided by them, so you'll have to figure out how to sell your products using other means.

Conclusions

CafePress is a great way to make money on the Internet if you've got some unique photography, art, drawings and so forth. You can build interesting merchandise using your own art or photographs and then sell them.

As with many of the options in this book, if you go this route you'll have to learn how to market and make your products known so that they can sell.

CDBaby

A friend of mine is a musician and he was looking for a place to sell his album. He settled on a service called CDbaby, which allowed him to create and upload an album of songs. There's a minimal cost to create the album, and once you designed a cover and uploaded all of the music, it is made available for sale.

CDbaby has its own storefront and is possible to make a few sales from people who visit the site and are browsing the music. However, more than likely you'll need to invest the time in marketing your album using various methods including email lists and advertising on music sites.

The website comes with the full suite of tools to enable you to create your album with as much music as you desire.

Pros

CDbaby is a great way to put your music, either singles or full albums, on the Internet for sale. Once you pay the fee and create your single or album, you can use CDbaby's storefront to make sales.

Cons

Creating an album is not free, although the cost is minimal. Unless you have a well-known brand, you'll have to spend time and money doing your own marketing to get people to purchase your music.

Conclusions

If you want to sell your music on the web, CDbaby is a great way to make that happen. While there is a charge to create an album or single, the amount is quite reasonable.

Craigslist

Recently I decided to declutter my home since I built up a huge collection of things over the years that I no longer needed. At first, I tried to sell my stuff on Amazon but quickly moved over to EBay because it is more suited to selling personal belongings that are in reasonably good condition.

While EBay is awesome for selling most merchandise, items that are heavy or bulky don't do as well because of shipping charges. For example, I have some large framed lithographs covered by glass, and the cost to have them professionally packed, so they won't break in transit, was about $35, and the shipping charge from UPS was $178. Since I was asking for $75 the lithograph, it wasn't surprising that I didn't make any sales.

Additionally, I have some larger items such as an exercise bike and furniture that I realized would definitely not be easily sold using EBay.

I turned to Craigslist and listed my lithographs, a few other framed pictures, the exercise bike and the furniture. The idea is that these items would be advertised locally, meaning the purchaser could pick up the items themselves, which eliminated shipping concerns.

Best of all? Listing on Craigslist is completely free.

Craigslist

Pros

Merchandise with a high shipping cost can be advertised on Craigslist and sold locally. This eliminates the problem of trying to ship bulkier heavy items. I found that merchandise tends to move quickly on Craigslist; there seems to be a lot of traffic to the site.

Cons

If you're not shipping the product, and your meeting somebody to exchange money for your merchandise, there is some risk involved. You're actually meeting a stranger face-to-face, so be careful and do so in a public place. Don't meet them at your home if you can avoid it.

Conclusions

Craigslist is a great way to sell merchandise. It has the advantage over Amazon and EBay in that listing items is completely free. However, if your meeting strangers in person to sell your merchandise, make sure you do so in a safe manner in a public place.

EBay

If you have accumulated large amounts of things throughout your life, or if a relative has recently passed away and left you with a lot of stuff that you want to get rid of, then EBay is an opportunity for you to make some decent money.

My book, *How to Sell on EBay*, tells you exactly how to sell stuff that you already own on EBay.

If you want to make money quickly and without a lot of bother, selling your own stuff on EBay makes perfect sense. All you need to do is create an EBay account, make a few small purchases to establish a reputation, and start selling.

At first, EBay will only allow you to list a few items, but as you prove yourself a reliable seller those limits will be increased you'll be able to sell more and more. Seller limits are EBay's way of keeping scammers from quickly opening accounts and ripping off a lot of people. This is because criminals don't generally want to take the time to establish themselves as reliable sellers.

There are other options available for selling including drop shipping and purchasing items which you then resell.

On EBay you can create stores will so your buyers can find all of your products together. You can check out my store at the EBayKing.

EBay

Pros

One of the primary advantages of using EBay is that you can sell stuff that you already own, as long as it's in reasonable condition. Since many people accumulate quite a few things over the lifetime, it's very possible that you have stuff that you no longer want that other people may be willing to buy.

Cons

EBay can be daunting as it has a large number of options and capabilities. For the beginner, there can be quite a learning curve to figure out how to get started listing their products. Additionally, selling limits placed on new accounts will keep the amount of money that you can make relatively low until you establish yourself as a reliable seller.

When selling on EBay, be sure you understand their fees and your shipping costs. Remember that packing materials, shipping tape, boxes, and envelopes cost you money and those need to be built into your charges.

Also, note that EBay is not a good place to sell larger or more bulky items due to shipping costs. See the section on Craigslist for more information.

Conclusions

Selling on EBay is a great place for someone new to Internet moneymaking to get started. While the interface can be daunting, with a little perseverance and a review of their help files, and reading my book *How to Sell on EBay*, it won't take long before you're selling your stuff and making some extra money.

Email Lists

Creating and building an email list is perhaps the most important and vital action that you can take if you want to make money on the Internet. Every other method of reaching your audience to make sales pales in comparison to the power and income generating possibilities of a targeted email list.

Building your own email list gives you contact information for people who were presumably interested enough in your products and services to give you permission to send them information.

To build an email list you need an autoresponder, such as TrafficWave or Aweber, to capture emails and send correspondence to the people on the list. Always use a double opt-in autoresponder, which means only those who request to be added to your list to get added, and they must confirm the addition by clicking a link in an email.

The second thing you need is a free, useful product which you give them as a thank you (or ethical bribe, as it sometimes called) for joining the list. A PDF file containing a checklist, an interview, or some other valuable information makes a great giveaway.

Use your autoresponder to set up timed emails to everyone on the list. I recommend you email them several times a week, perhaps even daily. The more you email them, the more money you will make — it really is that simple. Note that you will lose people from your list who don't want to receive that

Email Lists

many emails, but they're not going to purchase anything anyway so why worry about it?

Pros

In order to make any significant money on the Internet, you must create and maintain a highly targeted email list. Additionally, you must send out mailings to your list often, possibly even daily.

Cons

Creating and maintaining an email list is a lot of work. You have to create a free giveaway product (private label rights products are perfect for this), maintain an autoresponder (which generally will cost a monthly fee) and set up a few web pages on a web host.

Once you have the email list set up and ready to go, you must market it which means using targeted ads, another email list, social media, and other means to get people to see your free giveaway and sign up for your list.

Conclusions

Regardless of the amount of work it requires, setting up an email list is absolutely essential for making a significant income on the Internet. A general rule of thumb is if you don't have a targeted email list you are throwing money down the drain.

Etsy

Many of us enjoy hobbies of some kind. One of my friends, Elizabeth, likes to sew and knit. Another paints fantasy miniatures, and still another uses clay to create small necklaces other jewelry.

Using Etsy, you can expand your hobby into a business. Create an account, enter the information about each of your products - the things you create - into Etsy to make them available for others to purchase. The interface is straightforward and easy to learn.

Over the years, I've painted over a thousand fantasy miniatures. I decided it was time to thin down this collection, since my interest level was very low, and I settled on Etsy as the platform of choice for selling them. This worked very well and I was able to sell a good portion of my collection and make a few extra dollars.

While Etsy has a storefront and does do some marketing for you, you'll need to supplement it with marketing of your own in order to make sales. This could include paid Facebook, Twitter or Google ads as well as social media postings and email marketing. Basically, Etsy provides you with a storefront at your job to get buyers to see your products and make purchases.

It will take a little time to build up the following of people dedicated to your products, but the effort can pay off very well. As others begin to know you and your products, they will become dedicated followers of your store and make purchases of things that they find interesting or attractive.

In this case, it is absolutely essential to notify these people when you have new products to offer. You can do that via an email list or on social media with a business Facebook page.

Pros

Etsy provides an excellent interface allowing you to enter your product information, as well as a very good storefront. Payment is handled for you so you don't have to worry collecting money from your customers.

Cons

The fees for creating listings are quite high, and if your products are low-price or don't sell, you'll find yourself with low profits or even losing money. Additionally, unless you're in a very high-powered targeted niche, you'll need to do your own marketing to get people to your Etsy storefront.

Conclusions

If you'd like to turn a hobby into a moneymaking endeavor, you can't go wrong by choosing Etsy to sell your products. It is aimed precisely at the hobbyist who has created a business and they have provided a good set of tools for you to help you out in the process.

Fiverr

All that you need to get started on Fiverr is skill at something that others want or need and the time to do it. Just about any kind of service can be sold, including creating graphics, writing blogs, designing book covers, generating QR codes and so forth.

If you're interested in doing this, go take a look at Fiverr to see what others are offering. Match up those with your own skills and interests.

Once you find something that you like, make note of the prices, services, and descriptions that go along with it. Of course, if you have a unique service to offer you may not find it for sale on Fiverr.

The idea is to create gigs, which are basically brief consulting services. Each gig should be short and to the point. You need to be careful to make sure that you can do the task quickly and efficiently.

This is a very important point, as you don't want to charge $5 or $10 for something that takes you an hour or two. Even better, find tasks that you can automate.

For example, Photoshop has built in scripting, and you could take advantage of this to create scripts that generate graphics for people very quickly.

In the past, I purchased proofreading services from a lady who was attending college and needed some extra money. She created a gig and charged $5.00 for three thousand words of quality proofreading. After doing this for six months, she realized she was making about a dollar an hour and canceled the gig.

On the other hand, I created a gig to create QR codes, which are those funny looking barcodes that you scan with your smart phone to get information about a product. Using a service called QR Stuff, I was able to create these codes in a matter of minutes.

A good strategy is to create a basic service that is inexpensive, and then offer various add-ons which increase your profit. For example, there are many gigs to create book covers with add-ons such as providing the source copy so you can edit it yourself, allowing more revisions, or including a high-resolution graphic image. These additional services often don't require any more effort, are usually desired, and increase the amount of money you receive.

Pros

Fiverr is an excellent place to offer small, easy to create services that others desire. The interface is easy to use and the learning curve is very short. In general, you won't have to do much marketing yourself, other than promoting your gigs as best you can, because Fiverr is visited on a regular basis by people looking for services.

You don't have to worry about getting paid, because Fiverr demands payment upfront.

Cons

All communication with your customers must be done through the Fiverr interface. It is against the terms and conditions to ask for money outside of Fiverr, or communicate in any other way.

If you're not careful to understand how much time each of your tasks or gigs requires, you could find yourself not making as much income as you'd like, or spending an inordinate amount of time without making much income.

Fiverr does most of the marketing for you, since people visit the website looking for the service that they need.

Conclusions

The key to making an income on Fiverr is to offer services that are highly desired yet don't require a large amount of effort to get done. Additionally, you must ensure your description, optional services, and prices are all optimized to attract buyers.

As long as you keep these considerations in mind, and design your gigs appropriately, you shouldn't have any trouble making money providing services using Fiverr. You won't get rich, but you might be able to earn enough to pay off a few bills or go on vacation.

Freelance Writing

If you are a writer, you can make a good living doing freelance work for websites, online magazines, businesses, blogs, and so forth. There is work for writers everywhere, and literally, all you need to do is reach out and look for it.

This might seem obvious, but before you get started as a freelance writer, make sure you know how to write. Take a couple of courses — you can find a few good ones at Udemy — and learn the ropes not just about writing, but more specifically how to write for today's audience on the Internet.

You can set up gigs on Fiverr offering your writing services, or look for work on other consulting-type websites such as Contently or Upwork. Jobs on these websites are relatively low-paying but will give you experience at writing for customers and on the web.

It is difficult to make a living as a ghost-blogger because few people want to pay good rates to write a five hundred word article for their blog. You can certainly get low-paying gigs, but receiving decent pay for these tasks is difficult and requires building the appropriate reputation and credentials over a period of one or more years.

On the other hand, good copy for websites, emails, and other advertising medium is always in high demand, and these types of jobs can pay exceptionally good wages.

Freelance Writing

Pros

It is possible to make quite a good living as a freelance writer on the Internet. There is a virtually unlimited market for good writers all over the world.

Cons

Freelance writing can be highly competitive, and it can be frustrating losing bids and not being offered work, especially when you're just beginning. It's important to build a reputation and credibility, as well as a good portfolio of work you previously done, in order to get the larger, better pain jobs.

Conclusions

If you like to write, then you'll find plenty of work available on the Internet. You can write everything from advertising copy to blog articles to resumes and LinkedIn profiles. Writing well is a difficult skill to master, and there are many people in the world were willing to pay someone good rates to make use of the writing abilities.

Google Adsense

If you run a blog or a website, you may want to sign up for Google AdSense so you can display advertisements make a few extra dollars. Google will pay you a commission each time someone clicks on one of those ads.

Creating an AdSense account is very simple. Go to the Google AdSense page, create an account (if you don't already have one), and follow the instructions to set up your banner and text advertisements. Copy the HTML code into your website or blog and you're all set.

If you want to monetize other Google properties such as YouTube, then you'll need to set up an AdSense account anyway in order to collect your commissions.

Pros

Creating an AdSense account and putting advertisements on your blog or website is very simple and can make you some money now and then.

Cons

Unless you have a very high traffic blog or website, the amount of money you make will be trivial, possibly enough for dinner at a fast food restaurant every couple of months. Note that the minimum payout from Google is $100, which can take quite a bit of time to accumulate.

Conclusions

There is no harm in setting up a Google AdSense account, even if you don't put banner ads on your website or blog. Unless you have an exceptionally high traffic site, you probably are not going to make enough money to even pay for lunch.

JVZoo

JVZoo is a repository of products that other people have created which you can resell to earn income. You have at your fingertips thousands of different salable items, which include reports, moneymaking systems, courses, videos and so forth.

You can make use of this service in two ways. First, you can find products that you believe you can sell, request to become an affiliate, and then advertise those products in your social media, email list, and other means.

It is quite possible, if you put in the marketing effort, to make a pretty good living reselling these products.

If you create products of your own, you can list them on this website and other people will sell them for you. The idea is you design and package up something that is salable, such as a PDF report on how to make money from coloring books and create a listing on JVZoo. You determine the percentage of revenue that you will give to affiliates — sometimes as much as 50%.

The key to making this work is creating an excellent product, building the appropriate marketing materials, and convincing others to market your product for you. This may require that you reach out to marketers who have large email lists and make yourself known.

JVZoo

Pros

Signing up is simple, and there are plenty of products that you can resell in many different niches. If you put in the elbow grease, you can make a reasonable amount of money, especially if you can build (or get access to) a large, very targeted email list.

Cons

Many of the products included are of substandard quality, so you have to be careful about which you choose to promote so that you don't tarnish your own brand and image.

Creating a product for which there is a market can be quite a challenge, and you have to be prepared to do the hard work needed to network with the appropriate people to help you make sales.

Conclusions

JVzoo is an excellent place to find products that can work with your other business ventures. For example, if you write a book, you can include affiliate links to products that you recommend that go along with the subject of your manuscript. This can help leverage your readers so that you make more income than just the royalty amount.

Kickstarter

If you are a creative person and you have some ideas for projects, then check out Kickstarter. The idea is to crowd fund projects, which this means to get a lot of people to donate small amounts toward your goal. You create a page describing your project and offer various awards for differing levels of donations. You then work to get people to donate to your project, building up to the amount you need to get the funding.

For example, let's say you had an idea for an encyclopedia of dance choreographies and you estimate it will cost a thousand dollars to create and market the final product.

Once you have a budget set up a Kickstarter page. It is wise to add some padding to your budget because projects often cost more than anticipated. Define several levels of donations with a gift for each one. For the encyclopedia, you could offer a free digital copy for a $20 donation, a copy of the paperback for a $100 donation and perhaps a signed copy for a $250 donation.

A band producing an album might offer a backstage pass for a high donation, or even a night on the town with the band members for the highest level.

Believe it or not, lots people donate to these projects, and they become funded. Once the goal has been met, the creators receive the money. Note that in order to become funded, you must receive pledges equaling the entire amount or more. So

Kickstarter

if you ask for $1,000, you must receive at least $1,000 of pledges in order to receive the payout of $1,000.

Pros

There's no risk setting up a Kickstarter to fund your project. All it will cost you is the time necessary to create the kick starter page and to make that page known to your audience of fans and potential donors. Getting funded depends on how well you write up your kick starter, how well you market the idea, and the allure of the prizes offered for donations.

Cons

Getting a Kickstarter funded can be quite a bit of work, especially if you don't have a large fan base or know a number of people who are willing to donate to help your cause.

Conclusions

If you have a project that you want to fund, something creative such as a musical album, a book, a video game, or anything else artistic in nature, go ahead and create a Kickstarter campaign. It's relatively simple to set up, if you can get enough people to buy into the idea, you'll get the funding.

Private Label Rights

This is a very interesting idea which requires a bit of work on your part, but could pay off in the longer term. The concept is to purchase a product which you can resell under your own brand. These are called PLR, or Private Label Rights, products.

For example, I purchased a PLR product which consisted of a number of videos and a PDF document describing how to make money creating gigs on Fiverr. The package only cost me $2.97, and contained everything I needed to set up and market the product.

I had to load the videos online, set up the marketing funnel (which was included) on my web host, set up an email list on my autoresponder service, add my own labels and graphics, and start promoting the product. Oh yes, I also had to be sure to include my own affiliate code so that I would get paid.

This is a pretty simple way to get something to sell quickly. It does require the ability to set it up on a web host, define the autoresponder, set up the graphics and a few other skills. But the product has already been created so a big portion of the work is done for you.

Of course, the hard part is the marketing and convincing people to purchase it. You'll need to blast it out to an email list, if you have access to one, advertise it on your social media, and get the word out through your blog or website.

Private Label Rights

Pros

PLR products make it very easy to get started making money on the Internet. The product is already set up, including all the marketing funnels and such that you need to make it sell and collect email addresses. They also are generally very inexpensive, generally under $5.00, which is at a price point where you may as well purchase one or two to see if it works for you. Of course, the web hosting and autoresponder list may cost you more money – but you should get those anyway.

Cons

You will need to market the product, which means you'll need to build an email list, get some traffic to your website, purchase paid ads, and perform all the other usual actions needed to put your product in front of people. Marketing can be far more challenging than creating a product.

Additionally, PLR products tend to be popular and sometimes you may find the market is saturated, meaning those who need the product have already purchased it.

Conclusions

The beauty of PLR products is they are generally very inexpensive and contain useful, to the point courses or training which you may find a value. In fact, I bought several PLR products with the intention of simply taking the courses myself. Since there were only $2.97 each, I was able to get some very focused, useful training at a low price.

Sell Photos

If you are photographer or enjoy creating short videos, you can sell those to stock image sites such as Shutterstock or sell them yourself using either Zenfolio or SmugMug.

I am a photographer, and I've sold quite a few of my photographs using both Zenfolio and SmugMug. These two sites are roughly equivalent in function and price and allow you to store virtually unlimited numbers of photographs and videos in the cloud. They each have the ability to set prices and include a storefront, which is customizable, to help you sell your images.

As with most of the methods in this book, you must do the work to get visitors to your photography. This requires that you do your own marketing, or hire somebody to do it for you, and includes the usual techniques such as building email lists and creating a highly trafficked blog website.

On the other hand, submitting your photos to sites such as Shutterstock is much more straightforward. In this case, you create an account, become an affiliate, and if accepted, submit your photos. Those photos will go up on the Shutterstock website and be made available for searches and for sale. Several of my friends have submitted photos in this way and they have earned a nice income.

Sell Photos

Pros

Doing something you love, such as photography, and being able to sell it on the Internet is very rewarding and fulfilling. You can make a pretty good living selling your own pictures using the methods described above.

Cons

Whether or not you make money depends on how well you market your photography regardless of whether it's online or not. For stock photo sites, you don't need to do any marketing; you just load the photos up to the site and they do the selling for you. However, if you're going to sell them yourself you will need to learn marketing skills and get traffic with a targeted email list, a blog, or pay for advertisements.

Conclusions

If you're photographer, loading your images to a site such as Zenfolio or SmugMug makes sense. Other than the yearly fee, you have nothing to lose. If you can generate enough traffic you can make money from your photographs.

Selling your photos via stock image websites is also a great way to put those photographs to use to help you make an income.

Spreadshirt

If you have an idea for a t-shirt, then you might want to check out Spreadshirt. Create an account and either design and sell an individual shirt or open an online store to sell a number of your designs.

This is a great option for you if you are an artist and want to make a few extra dollars selling t-shirts of your own creation.

Best of all, the shirts are print-on-demand, meaning you don't have to keep any inventory or pay production costs. Instead, shirts are created (printed) as they are ordered by customers.

Pros

All shirts are printed on demand as they are ordered. The website handles payment and maintains your custom storefront.

Cons

You'll have to generate traffic to your storefront using email lists, paid advertisements, and other means.

Conclusions

This website is a great way to make some extra cash from art that you've created. Since there is no charge (except for your time) you should definitely check it out.

Thumbtack

Thumbtack is similar to Upwork in that it helps you find consulting jobs. The difference is that Upwork takes a cut of your consulting fee while on Thumbtack you pay to make a bid.

Any kind of job can be found on Thumbtack. You could find a local photographer in your area to do head shots, a clown who will come to your house and perform at your children's birthday party, or mechanic for your car.

Customers request bids stating what service they need, and consultants, or pros as they are called, respond to those with proposals and the amount of money they want to charge for the service.

The key to winning proposals on Thumbtack is to bid quickly and low. Generally, I found the customers are looking to spend the smallest amount of money possible.

Since you're paying for the privilege of bidding, you want to make sure that you're not losing money by consistently delivering bids that don't get accepted.

Pros

Thumbtack delivers quite a bit of work if you're quick on the reply and you're willing to be the lowest bidder.

Thumbtack

Cons

You have to be careful with this website, because you can burn through a lot of money very quickly if you continually lose bids. Also, I found the jobs tend to be of lower quality, meaning less desirable, than sites like Upwork.

Conclusions

If you use Thumbtack wisely, or if you're in a narrow niche, you can probably make a decent amount of money using this website. This is especially true if you're willing to perform consulting jobs cheaply.

Udemy

If you're one of those people who like to teach others, then you'll find Udemy to be a good choice for making income on the Internet. This site offers tens of thousands of courses at reasonable costs on virtually every subject imaginable.

These courses are usually tightly focused on solving specific problems and are generally short and low cost. Udemy often runs specials, meaning they may sometimes go as low as $7 to $10 per course. This makes it an ideal place for people to purchase quick and easy training that they need to do in a hurry without spending a lot of money,

On the other side of the coin, Udemy offers a full suite of tools and training to enable individuals to create courses. In order to create training, you have to write a script, create some presentations if needed, and shoot a few videos.

The training provided by Udemy is high quality and walks you through exactly what you need to do to create a course. It's definitely a lot of work; creating even a short course of an hour will take a significant amount of time, especially the first or second time through.

However, Udemy markets courses heavily to supplement any marketing efforts that you're doing. So you will most likely, depending on the quality of your course and the popularity of the niche, get customers and make a few dollars. If your niche is correctly targeted and you create enough quality courses, you can find yourself with a nice income.

Udemy

The beauty of the whole process is you can create as many courses as you like. A standard course is only an hour or so long, and may consist of 20 to 30 videos, each of only two to three minute duration. Build a few videos each day, add a few checklists and other downloads, and within a short time you've got a course.

Once you got one course done, start on a second, and then a third. Build a series of courses that relate to each other so that when a person buys one course they may be willing to purchase the rest of them.

Courses work especially well as an upsell from a cheaper product or book. The way this works is you write a book and sell it normally on a site such as Amazon. At the end of the book offer something free, a special report, for example, to sign up to an email list. Once there on that list, offer them products such as your courses. This is known as a marketing funnel and is a very effective way to add more income and build a product line.

Pros

Udemy is a great way to build courses which you can sell and make it income. They provide excellent training modules on how to go through the process and have marketing front end to help sell your courses. A properly targeted niche has the potential to make you some income.

Cons

Creating a course can be daunting, and is certainly a lot of work. If the niche is not properly targeted, you may find yourself doing a lot of work and not making a lot of money.

Conclusions

I find creating courses to be very fulfilling because it's a great way to teach people how to do something. Udemy gives you all the tools that you need to get the job done. Courses work very well as an add on or upsell to books or other products.

Upwork

There are number websites that allow you to find consulting work, and Upwork is one of the best of those. Once you define your profile on the site you can use their search engine to find consulting jobs, and then submit proposals and bids to try and land that work.

This is a great place to find consulting jobs. The listings are very active, making it useful to check it out every day. Unfortunately, many of the jobs are fairly low quality, small, and tend to go to the lowest bidder. That being said, you will occasionally run across a good gig and make a little money.

Pros

The job listings are very active, which means that you have a good chance of finding something that you can do to earn money.

All payment is handled through the website, which relieves you of the necessity of trying to get paid.

Cons

Upwork charges a 20% fee for jobs under five hundred dollars, but that percentage goes down as the value of the job increases.

Competition for consulting jobs can be quite intense, and often the job will be awarded to the lowest bidder. Don't get discouraged, just keep making proposals, and sometimes you will get the bid.

<u>Conclusions</u>

If you're looking for a way to make money, then you'll find Upwork to be a useful tool. At the very least, if you're interested in consulting at all, create a profile and take a look every once in a while to see if there any gigs that that are of interest. You will occasionally run across one that makes sense and can earn you a little bit of income.

Virtual Assistant

If you have extra time - even if you don't have many skills - and a computer connected to the Internet, you can become a virtual assistant. This consists of performing various tasks for someone in return for a fee.

These tasks include creating a spreadsheet, compiling data, researching something on the Internet, creating reports, or just about anything else that you can imagine that can be done from a distance.

There are many websites where you can set yourself up as a virtual assistant and make it known that you are willing to provide services to others. I've found several good virtual assistants using Fiverr who were able to help me by doing research for creating spreadsheets.

In one case, I sent a thousand emails to a virtual assistant and paid $10 for her to extract certain information from each email and put it together in a spreadsheet. In another instance, I was writing an article and needed some research about the subject done via Google very quickly. I hired a virtual assistant to do that research and compile a report of what they found.

Becoming a virtual assistant is a great way to get started making income on the Internet. No matter your skill set, you can find someone who's willing to pay for your time to do something that they'd rather not do themselves.

Virtual Assistant

Pros

Becoming a virtual assistant generally doesn't require more than simple computer and data entry skills. The tasks that you can perform to help others are virtually endless, and if you're lucky enough to find a few steady customers, you can make a lot of money.

Cons

Due to the nature of the competition, virtual assistance don't tend to make a lot of money per hour. Unless you have a very specialized talent or niche, you will probably top out at the $15 to $20 rate.

One of the difficulties of setting yourself up in this business is you are competing against individuals and shops in other countries who have much lower income requirements. It's not uncommon for someone in Pakistan or India to be the lowest bidders on projects.

Conclusions

If you got some time available, becoming a virtual assistant is a good way to make a little extra money. Most likely you are not going to become rich being a virtual assistant, but with a little work and some good marketing, the income you create could help pay the bills or make life a little bit easier.

Before starting, make sure you have a good grasp of computer skills and can use both Microsoft Word and Excel without much effort. Quite a few of the jobs that you get will involve creating documents or spreadsheets, or performing searches on the Internet.

Warrior+

Similar in concept to JVZoo, Warrior+ gives you a list of thousands of products that you can resell, and you can create your own products and convince others to sell them as affiliates.

This is a whole different market than trying to sell books or other products on websites such as Amazon or EBay. Warrior+ tends to attract buyers who are interested in making money, and they are looking for products that will help them achieve that goal.

Some of these products can help you earn more income while others are quite simply scams or are largely ineffective. Keep in mind that products sold on this website can be very lucrative, so it's not uncommon for individuals to quickly pump out new things to sell on a regular basis.

Pros

There are a lot of products to choose from, and some of them can make you quite a bit of money. Additionally, if you create a product of your own, especially if it is related to moneymaking, then you can use this platform to sell it.

Cons

Carefully evaluate a product before you offer it for sale as an affiliate. I have run across quite a few offerings from Warrior+ which are outright scams, such as pyramid schemes, or which are very low quality.

Conclusions

Warrior+ is one of those websites that you should keep an eye on but proceed with caution on any purchases. Keep in mind that these products, and especially the marketing copy associated with them, are designed to attract people who are desperate for ways to make income. The products generally tend to be relatively cheap, usually under $10 each, but have more expensive upsells to deliver more value (or just more expensive options.)

Occasionally, you'll run across a gem that you can resell to make a little income for yourself. These products can work very well as add-ons to existing books, products and services that you are selling.

Writing and Publishing Books

An interesting way to make money on the Internet is to write (or hire someone to ghostwrite) and publish books. With huge shopping sites such as Amazon, Barnes & Noble and iBook, there's plenty of markets for just about anything you care to put into words.

There are many options for publishing your own books, and there are hundreds, if not thousands, of training courses available. One of the best ones for Kindle nonfiction books is Author Audience Academy. In this series of courses, Shelley Hitz gives you everything you need to know about Kindle nonfiction e-books from beginning to end.

Perhaps the easiest option is to write a book, fiction or non-fiction, and upload it to KDP, which is the publishing website for Amazon. You can also publish your book, again on Amazon, in paperback or audiobook formats.

If you want, you can take advantage of publishers such as IngramSpark to publish your book in hardcover format and you can use Babelcube to translate your book into as many as ten different languages. Additionally, sites such as SmashWords and Draft2Digital can be used to get your book onto other platforms such as iBook, the nook, and so forth.

Pros

If you are a creative person with a bent toward writing, then there is nothing that will give you satisfaction like seeing your book in print (or the electronic equivalent.)

Writing and Publishing Books

Once you've written your book, you have a wide variety of options to help you get it published and selling. If you produce a quality book on the subject in which other people are interested and work very hard to market it to the right audience, you can certainly earn yourself a few extra dollars, and perhaps even a living.

Cons

Because self-publishing is very simple and free on many platforms, the market is saturated – actually, beyond saturated – with books. Over 6,500 different volumes are published every single day on Amazon and thousands more in the other publishing houses.

With that kind of volume of materials being created and published, marketing your books becomes essential. Unless you're very lucky, you'll need to create an email list, purchase paid ads, create a blog, and do a number of other things in order to get people to look at and possibly purchase what you've written.

Even though it might appear that writing a book is difficult, getting people to actually purchase the book is several orders of magnitude harder.

Conclusions

There are many reasons to write a book, and not all of them are financial in basis. You might want to get your message known, build your personal brand, explain your genealogy, or define your ideas.

Writing and Publishing Books

Amazon and other publishing houses make it trivial for you to publish the books that you have written. The difficulty lies in "getting eyeballs" to those books so that purchases can be made.

As a professional bestselling author, I've learned a bit about how to market books and am learning more every single day. It's important for anyone venturing down this path to understand that it is not a game for the weak of heart. However, with enough effort and a solid focus on marketing, you can make a good living writing, publishing and selling your own books.

YouTube Videos

If you enjoy creating videos, then you'll be excited by the opportunity to make money on YouTube. Since YouTube is owned by Google, you'll need to also create a Google AdSense account in order to get paid.

People put up all kinds of videos on YouTube, and some of the strangest things become popular. Humorous videos seem to generate a lot of views, but even something as seemingly boring as how to unpack a product can become very popular and well-known.

After you open a YouTube account and connect it to your Google AdSense account, you need to create videos. You can do this using your smart phone, a digital camera with video capability, or a professional camera. Higher quality is better since that produces cleaner videos which give your viewers a better experience.

You'll have to authorize your account for monetization, and once you do that you be able to upload short videos.

YouTube will automatically add advertisements to the videos and you will receive a small amount of money each time somebody views those ads.

All of this can be a little complex to set up, but there is plenty of help available online to give you instructions.

Youtube scans each video for copyright infringements, such as the use of music that is owned by someone else. If it finds something it recognizes, YouTube will use its contract with the copyright owner to decide how to treat your video. In some instances, it will allow the infringement but all monies will go to the copyright owner, and others it will remove the soundtrack or block the video in certain countries.

Pros

If your videos become popular, you can make quite a bit of money. Some of the more popular channels, which get millions of hits per month, actually make their owners a good living.

After you get through the initial set up, which is a little cumbersome, adding new videos is relatively simple and straightforward. You can even edit them online using tools available from YouTube.

Cons

Creating a video that generates enough views to make an income of any significance can be challenging, especially for someone who is not a professional. Building an audience doesn't happen overnight unless you are already well known, and most videos receive views that are in the dozens or hundreds rather than in the tens of thousands per day better that is needed to make a decent income.

Conclusions

If you like creating videos, then you'll enjoy sharing them with others on YouTube. If you can find an audience, or if you already have one, then you can certainly make a decent amount of money. Unfortunately, most videos only generate enough views to pay out pennies at a time.

Conclusion

You can make a living working from home and use the Internet in various programs as described in this book. Of course, there are far more methods and websites than I've discussed here. My purpose was to give you a good selection of different methods to make money to give you some ideas you can pursue on your own.

Keep in mind that you probably won't make enough to replace her full-time job right away. In fact, you may feel a little disappointed at the amount that you're making when you start this journey. But if you keep putting in the effort, and are willing to experiment and receive training, you'll probably find that it becomes easier and easier. However, I would highly recommend that you don't quit your day job until you create an Internet business that generates the income you need.

It is also important to understand that you are creating a business and you need to treat it as such. Keep good records, pay your taxes — including local, state and federal — and make sure you have the appropriate business license from the locality where your business is located. If you are reselling products, then you'll need a tax license from your state – assuming your state collects sales tax – and you'll have to pay them as well.

And as a self-employed person, don't forget about self-employment tax. Your accountant will be able to tell you more about this. If you start making a sizable income, you'll probably want to incorporate.

Conclusion

One of the cool things about working from home is you can get a large number of income tax deductions that were unavailable to you when you work for someone else. Be sure and check with your tax accountant for details; in many cases you can deduct part of your home is a home office, a percentage of your car if you use it for business purposes, payments to medical insurance and so forth.

Don't let any of that discourage you or prevent you from getting started. My advice is to jump right in to whichever method seems appropriate for your passion, and begin making some extra income. Keep good records of any income and expenses and you'll be fine.

I have found that working from home, which lets me pursue my passions, is an order of magnitude more fulfilling than working for a business or another person. I have the option of choosing the jobs that I want to pursue, the types of work that I want to do, and the products that I want to create.

It's an amazing feeling standing back and looking at, in my case, the books that I have published on Amazon and realizing that I was the one who flowed my passions into those books and succeeded in creating them. Not only that, but I've been able to make a good income doing so.

This is a much more fulfilling way to spend my life than sitting in an office, dreading that visit from the boss, worrying over the yearly review, or getting that unexpected call at 2am from a micromanaging supervisor. There is no longer a two hour grueling commute to and from the office, and I no longer feel the stress of being on call 24 x 7, 365 days a year. I don't need to attend countless pointless meetings and no longer have mindless discussions with the boss and staff.

Best of all, I don't have to work for a boss that I can't respect or a management structure that doesn't care.

I am now responsible for my own destiny in a much more direct manner. My income depends on my skills and the quality of the products and services that I create, as well as my success at marketing those products and services.

I call this "the writing life," but you could just as well call it "the artist life" or the "virtual assistant's life."

Of course on the other side of the coin, my income is directly related to my ability to produce products and services, and to convince other people to purchase them. That's one of the advantages of working for someone else — they are responsible for billing, taxes, office space, and countless other details. All of those things are now my concern.

The reality is that even though we may feel safe in our job, and think we will be working there forever, each of us could be laid off or fired at any time. Regardless of the law, if your boss doesn't like you or the company makes a bad decision, you could easily be the target of a layoff or firing.

Being one's own boss and being responsible for your own income is not for everyone. It's a daunting task, especially at the beginning when you're setting it all up. But as long as you're willing to reach out for help when you need it, get trained as appropriate, and change course and direction if need be, you'll probably do fine.

Conclusion

And even if you aren't looking to work from home on a full-time basis, you'll find many of the services and websites mentioned in this book will be useful to creating a part-time income or at least to supplement to your paycheck.

Good luck on your journey.

Before you go

If you scroll to the last page in this eBook, you will have the opportunity to leave feedback and share the book with Before You Go. I'd be grateful if you turned to the last page and shared the book.

Also, if you have time, please leave a review. Positive reviews are incredibly useful. If you didn't like the book, please email me at rich@thewritingking.com and I'd be happy to get your input.

TAKE CONTROL OF YOUR PERSONAL BRAND **ON LINKEDIN**

Interviews with Influencers Series #4

An Interview with Richard G Lowe Jr, Senior Branding Expert and Bestselling Author of Focus on LinkedIn

Richard G Lowe Jr

Learn how to use LinkedIn to get more and better qualified leads

Click the link for your free eBook and to sign up for tips

linkedin.thewritingking.com

linkedin.thewritingking.com

About the Author

https://www.linkedin.com/in/richardlowejr
Feel free to send a connection request

Follow me on Twitter: @richardlowejr

Richard Lowe has leveraged more than 35 years of experience as a Senior Computer Manager and Designer at four companies into that of a bestselling author, blogger, ghostwriter, and public speaker. He has written hundreds of articles for blogs and ghostwritten more than a dozen books and has published manuscripts about computers, the Internet, surviving disasters, management, and human rights. He is currently working on a ten-volume science fiction series – the Peacekeeper Series – to be published at the rate of three volumes per year, beginning in 2016.

Richard started in the field of Information Technology, first as the Vice President of Consulting at Software Techniques, Inc. Because he craved action, after six years he moved on to work for two companies at the same time: he was the Vice President of Consulting at Beck Computer Systems and the Senior Designer at BIF Accutel. In January 1994, Richard found a home at Trader Joe's as the Director of Technical Services and Computer Operations. He remained with that incredible company for almost 20 years before taking an early retirement to begin a new life as a professional writer. He is currently the CEO of The Writing King, a company that provides all forms of writing services, the owner of The EBay King, and a Senior Branding Expert for LinkedIn Makeover. You can find a current list of all books on his Author Page and

About the Author

take a look at his exclusive line of coloring books at <u>The Coloring King</u>.

Richard has a quirky sense of humor and has found that life is full of joy and wonder. As he puts it, "This little ball of rock, mud, and water we call Earth is an incredible place, with many secrets to discover. Beings fill our corner of the universe, and some are happy, and others are sad, but each has their unique story to tell."

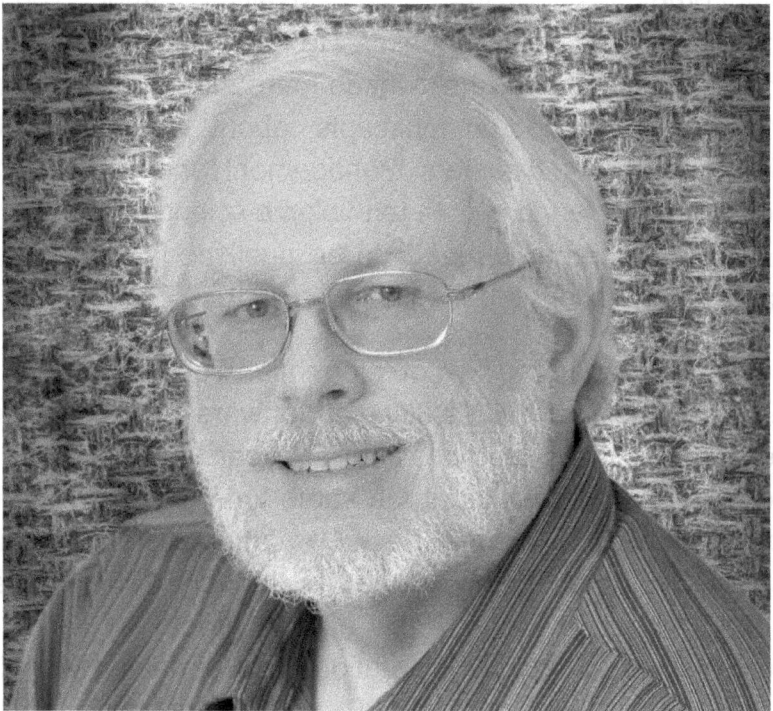

His philosophy is to take life with a light heart, and he approaches each day as a new source of happiness. Evil is ignored, discarded, or defeated; good is helped, enriched, and fulfilled. One of his primary interests is to educate people about their human rights and assist them to learn how to be happy in life.

Richard spent many happy days hiking in national parks, crawling over boulders, and peering at Indian pictographs. He toured the Channel Islands off Santa Barbara and stared in fascination at wasps building their homes in Anza-Borrego. One of his joys is photography, and he has photographed more than 1,200 belly dancing events, as well as dozens of Renaissance fairs all over the country.

Because writing is his passion, Richard remains incredibly creative and prolific; each day he writes between 5,000 and 10,000 words, diligently using language to bring life to the world so that others may learn and be entertained.

Richard is the CEO of The Writing King, which specializes in fulfilling any writing need. You can find out more at https://www.thewritingking.com/, and emails are welcome at rich@thewritingking.com

Books by Richard G Lowe Jr.

Business Professional Series

On the Professional Code of Ethics and Business Conduct in the Workplace – Professional Ethics: 100 Tips to Improve Your Professional Life - have you ever wondered what it takes to be successful in the professional world? This book gives you some tips that will improve your job and your career.

Help! My Boss is Whacko! - How to Deal with a Hostile Work Environment - sometimes the problem is the boss. There are all kinds of managers, some competent, some incompetent, and others just plain whacked. This book will help you understand and handle those different types of managers.

Help! I've Lost My Job: Tips on What to do When You're Unexpectedly Unemployed – suddenly having to leave your job can be a harsh and emotional time in your life. Learn some of the things that you need to consider and handle if this happens to you.

Help! My Job Sucks Insider Tips on Making Your Job More Satisfying and Improving Your Career – sometimes conditions conspire to make the regular trek to a job feel like a trip through Dante's Inferno. Sometimes, these are out of our control, such as a malicious manager or incompetent colleague. On the other hand, we can take control of our lives and workplace and improve our situation. Get this book to learn what you can do when your job sucks.

Books by Richard G Lowe Jr.

How to Manage a Consulting Project: Make money, get your project done on time, and get referred again and again – I found that being a consultant is a great way to earn a living. Managing a consulting project can be a challenge. This book contains some tips to help you so you can deliver a better product or service to your customers.

How to be a Good Manager and Supervisor, and How to Delegate – Lessons Learned from the Trenches: Insider Secrets for Managers and Supervisors – I've been a manager for over thirty years I learned many things about how to get the job done and deliver quality service. The information in this book will help you manage your projects to a high level of quality.

Focus on LinkedIn – Learn how to create a LinkedIn profile and to network effectively using the #1 business social media site.

Home Computer Security Series

Safe Computing is Like Safe Sex: You have to practice it to avoid infection – Security expert and Computer Executive, Richard Lowe, presents the simple steps you can take to protect your computer, photos and information from evil doers and viruses. Using easy-to-understand examples and simple explanations, Lowe explains why hackers want your system, what they do with your information, and what you can do to keep them at bay. Lowe answers the question: how to you keep yourself say in the wild west of the internet.

Books by Richard G Lowe Jr.

<u>Disaster Preparation and Survival Series</u>

<u>Real World Survival Tips and Survival Guide: Preparing for and Surviving Disasters with Survival Skills</u> – CERT (Civilian Emergency Response Team) trained and Disaster Recovery Specialist, Richard Lowe, lays out how to make you, your family, and your friends ready for any disaster, large or small. Based upon specialized training, interviews with experts and personal experience, Lowe answers the big question: what is the secret to improving the odds of survival even after a big disaster?

<u>Creating a Bug Out Bag to Save Your Life: What you need to pack for emergency evacuations</u> - When you are ordered to evacuate—or leave of your free will—you probably won't have a lot of time to gather your belongings and the things you'll need. You may have just a few minutes to get out of your home. The best preparation for evacuation is to create what is called a bug out bag. These are also known as go-bags, as in, "grab it and go!"

<u>Professional Freelance Writer Series</u>

<u>How to Operate a Freelance Writing Business, and How to be a Ghostwriter – Proven Tips and Tricks Every Author Needs to Know about Freelance Writing: Insider Secrets from a Professional Ghostwriter</u> – This book explains how to be a ghostwriter, and gives tips on everything from finding customers to creating a statement of work to delivering your final product.

<u>How to Write a Blog That Sells and How to Make Money From Blogging: Insider Secrets from a Professional Blogger:</u>

Books by Richard G Lowe Jr.

<u>Proven Tips and Tricks Every Blogger Needs to Know to Make Money</u> – There is an art to writing an article that prompts the reader to make a decision to do something. That's the narrow focus of this book. You will learn how to create an article that gets a reader interested, entices them, informs them, and causes them to make a decision when they reach the end.

Other Books by Richard Lowe Jr

How to Be Friends with Women: How to Surround Yourself with Beautiful Women without Being Sleazy – I am a photographer and frequently find myself surrounded by some of the most beautiful women in the world. This book explains how men can attract women and keep them as friends, which can often lead to real, fulfilling relationships.

How to Throw Parties like a Professional: Tips to Help You Succeed with Putting on a Party Event – Many of us have put on parties, and I know it can be a daunting and confusing experience. In this book, I share what I learned from hosting small house parties to shows and events.

Additional Resources

Is your career important to you? Find out how to move your career in any direction you desire, improve your long-term livelihood, and be prepared for any eventuality. Visit the page below to sign up to receive valuable tips via email, and to get a free eBook about how to optimize your LinkedIn profile.

http://list.thewritingking.com/

I've written and published many books on a variety of subjects. They are all listed on the following page.

https://www.thewritingking.com/books/

On that site, I also publish articles about business, writing, and other subjects. You can visit by clicking the following link:

https://www.thewritingking.com

To find out more about me or my photography, you can visit these sites:

Personal website: https://www.richardlowe.com
Photography: http://www.richardlowejr.com
LinkedIn Profile: https://www.linkedin.com/in/richardlowejr
Twitter: https://twitter.com/richardlowejr

If you have any comments about this book, feel free to email me at rich@thewritingking.com

Premium Writing Services

Do you have a story that needs to be told? Have you been trying to write a book for ages but never can seem to find the time to get it done? Do you want to brand your business, but don't know how to get started?

The Writing King has the answer. We can help you with any of your writing needs.

Ghostwriting. We can write your book, which entails interviewing you to get your story, writing the book and then working with you to revise it until complete. To discuss your book, contact The Writing King today.

Website Copy. Many businesses include the text on their sites as an afterthought, and that can result in lost sales and leads. Hire The Writing King to review your site and recommend changes to the text which will help communicate your message and improve your sales.

Blogging. Build engagement with your customers by hiring us to write a weekly or semi-weekly article for your blog, LinkedIn or other social media. Contact The Writing King today to discuss your blogging needs.

LinkedIn. LinkedIn is of the most important vehicles for finding new business, and a professionally written profile works to pulling in those leads. Write or update your profile today.

Technical Writing. We have broad experience in the computer, warehousing and retail industries, and have

Premium Writing Services

written hundreds of technical documents. Contact The Writing King today to find out how we can help you with your technical writing project.

The Writing King has the skills and knowledge to help you with any of your writing needs. Call us today to discuss how we can help you.

www.ingramcontent.com/pod-product-compliance
Lightning Source LLC
Chambersburg PA
CBHW071716210326
41597CB00017B/2506